STEP OUTSIDE YOUR STORY

A Journey of Discovery

JOHN DRURY

Published in 2012 by
FullyAlive360, Inc
drury@fullyalive360.com

Edited by Matt Sacco and Sharon Gelfano
Design and layout by Socrates Gomez
Soul Questions photography by Socrates Gomez

First Edition
ISBN number 0-9776985-2-1
Printed in Canada

John Drury
john@insideoutedge.com
954.444.3460
www.insideoutedge.com
www.insideoutedgeinstitute.com

This book is dedicated to my wife Debbie.
I am the man I am today because of her
love and commitment to our marriage.
37 years and counting.

STEP OUTSIDE YOUR STORY

Contents

INTRODUCTION

Most of us are not living the life we are meant to live.

We are living the life our story tells us to live.

I see it all the time. People struggle to live a life of passion and love
because they are stuck in their story.

We all have stories we tell ourselves about ourselves.
Every human action is in some way an expression of how we think about ourselves.

These stories become the framework – healthy or not – that we live within.

We believe these stories to be true. Even when they are not.

Today my life's work is to help people examine these stories that drive their behavior.

I've heard thousands of stories in my retreats and coaching work.
I have heard stories of celebration, pain, loss, transition, abuse, love,
betrayal and much more. In this book, I'll share many of these stories
to give you insight into how they can be both a gift and a block.

Our stories are born from early childhood
experiences and they become the lens through which
we see the world. They are snapshots of who we are. They are a composite of past
experiences and the input of outsiders – both the good and the questionable.

These stories often leave us conflicted. We give them heed and trust when they tell us what to do, what to be, how to live, how to dress, who we are, and who we aren't. **We listen when they tell us what's right, even when we feel it might be wrong.**

I created this book to give you some insight into how your story is created, how it impacts your life and what you can do to change it.

Our story has many layers including our fears, emotional wounds, beliefs, values and unconscious commitments. The book is broken down into these layers to show you how they become the defining chapters of our story - and how they work on us.

The artwork in the book is designed to help you reflect and think about your life at a deeper level. **We must take the time to reflect and examine those parts of us, digging through the defenses that play a significant role in creating our life and impacting the choices we make every day.**

At the end of each layer, I've created 'Soul Questions' to support and deepen the process. Take the time to answer the questions thoughtfully. Only by becoming conscious of the story we are telling ourselves can we strive to regain our life's direction.

This book is full of color and paint! Why? Well, you've heard the expression "every painting tells a story". I believe that's true and **we are here on this earth to paint our own masterpiece, our own story.** **Not the one our mom, dad and others want us to paint.** But a masterpiece that is uniquely ours. Throughout the book I've used this metaphor as a reminder for you to live more colorfully and passionately; to paint your own masterpiece by examining your story.

It is time to end the story we've been telling ourselves; the story that keeps us from creating a life we deserve, a life that is undeniably ours.

Time to step outside your story.

1

OUR STORY

Layer 1

OUR STORY

Our story is the framework for our life.

It is an important part of how we grow up and survive in our world.
Our story is our comfort zone. Our story attempts to keep us safe.

When our environment offers challenges, and danger, and risk,
we return to our story for comfort and direction.

It is possible to get too comfortable. Like railway tracks, our story keeps us moving forward regardless
of the terrain. Subconsciously, our life follows the track laid down by our upbringing and our experiences.

What happens when we **want to change direction?**

What happens when we want to lose weight, change careers,
try a different lifestyle, take up a new challenge, or find
a new relationship? Our story may not allow it.
It may put up blinders to the unfamiliar
and sabotage our dreams.

We must step outside of our story.

At one of my workshops I met Bill, a 35-year-old man frustrated with his inability to follow through
both personally and professionally. He often attempts to **execute changes** in his life that
are important to him, such as

losing weight, quitting smoking and starting a new business. For some reason, **he is never able to see it through to the end.**

As an example, Bill sets a goal to lose 25 lbs. He creates a nutrition plan and a workout regimen and follows it to the letter for about two weeks before things start to unravel. He begins to make excuses for missing workouts or eating poorly and finds himself back at square one: **unfinished, unfulfilled and controlled by the same old story.**

The same situation occurs when he attempts to stop smoking, or start a new business, or start a new relationship.

The challenge for Bill is that in order to overcome his inability to follow through, he has to examine his story.

Bill grew up with parents who were educators. His sister was an "A" student while he was a "C" student. The effort was there, **but no matter how hard he tried**, Bill could not muster the same success as his sister, the success his parents expected.

His parents only cared about the end result.

They didn't care about the effort; all they cared about was the grade on the report card.

When Bill realized "trying hard" was never going **to be good enough,** he began to sabotage his efforts and make excuses because subconsciously, he thought, "no matter how hard I try, it's not going to make a difference."

This is Bill's story, it subconsciously prevents him from **expressing himself properly** and experiencing life to the fullest. It is what prevents him from reaching his goals or seeing things through to the end. ◼

It hampered him when he was eight-years-old and it hinders him now that he is 35.

The difference now is he has **stepped out of his story** and examined it.

He now realizes how his story can **hold him back**. Talking about his story openly has given him a recognition he never had before. And once he took a step back and looked at his story for the first time, his reaction was quite simply, "holy shit."

This recognition gave Bill the freedom to overcome the limitations his story had put on him

and the ability to live a life that is more fully alive.

To find that awareness, as Bill has, we must take the time to look at the experiences that shaped our life and ask ourselves some difficult questions.

Unfortunately, many of us try to avoid these questions by staying busy.

We may not want to face the truth when asking ourselves:

Am I happy with my life?

Am I doing what I love to do? Am I missing out?

Why am I so busy all the time?

I have a friend who possesses an incredible gift to mentor others, but he is so caught up in deal making and going 100 miles per hour while working himself to the bone, he completely ignores this gift. However, **when he slows down and pays attention** to it, he feels an incredible amount of emotional fulfillment, while also reaping financial dividends well beyond his deal making.

His story is simple: in order to survive and avoid pain, he has to stay busy.

As a youngster, he and his brother were emotionally and physically abused by parents who fought all the time and a father who would **release his anger on his sons**. He couldn't fight back, so instead, he would **pack his days with chores and responsibilities** to keep him away from the house and thus, out of dad's wrath. When he was home, **he went out of his way to do things that kept both of his parents happy,** to keep the abuse at bay.

He kept busy to avoid the pain. His busyness served him very well.

Fast forward to adulthood and he is still excessively busy,
and has been very successful because of it.

On the other hand, he's so busy that his life is passing him by.
He's missing his life and missing the opportunity to express his gifts.

Our stories are like a double-edged sword. On one side, there can be a gift in it and on the other, it can **sabotage our life.**

My friend took the time to examine his story and realized he has a powerful
gift to create success in his life because of his incredible work ethic.

But he also learned if he slows down and mentors others,
he enjoys his life at a much deeper level.

Every person has a story. Yes, we are individuals. Yes, we are unique.
But we all have ingredients and experiences – both positive and negative – that shape our story.
In the end, we all face the same challenge our stories create for us.

No one is immune.

Step outside your story. **Investigate yourself.**

Take the time to analyze the lens through which you see
the world and **the filter through which you process your life.**

The first step is awareness and the result is
a life that is more fully alive. ▶

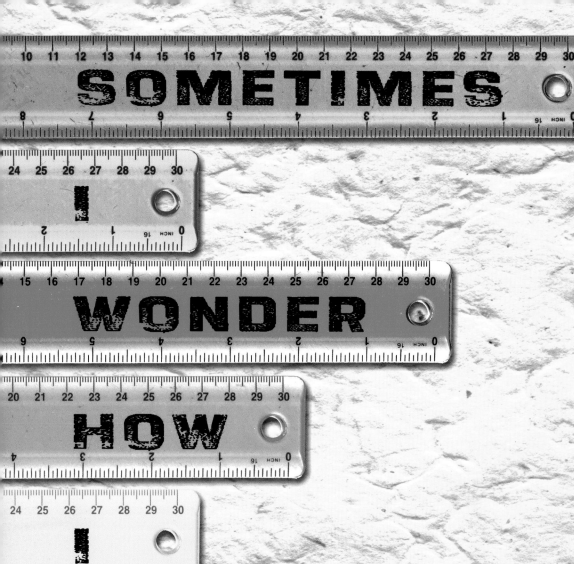

SOMETIMES
I
WONDER
HOW
I
MEASURE
UP

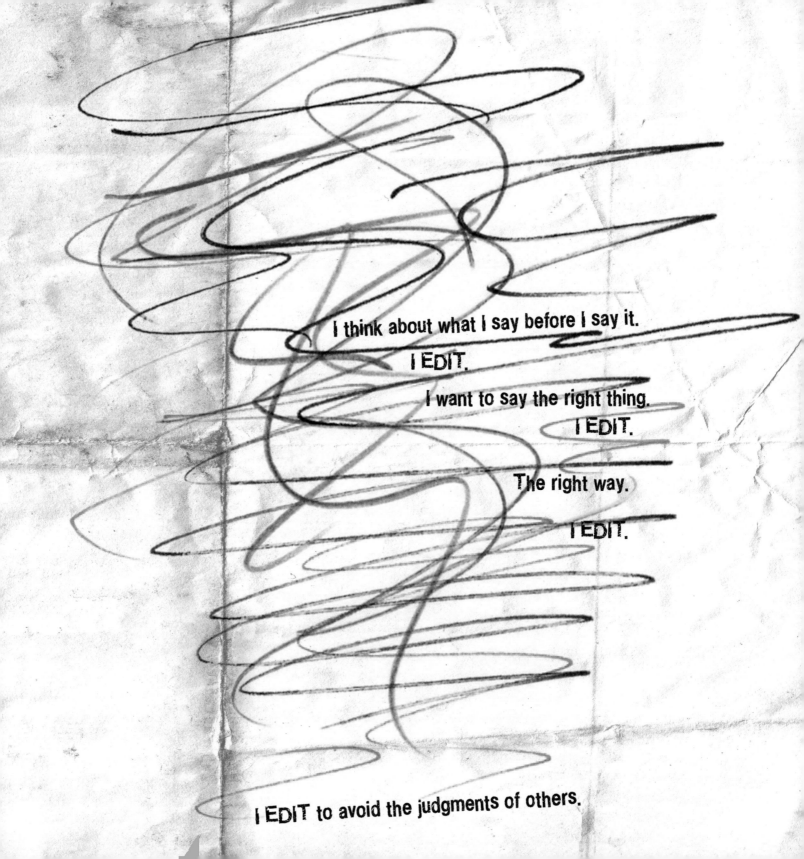

I think about what I say before I say it.

I EDIT.

I want to say the right thing.

I EDIT.

The right way.

I EDIT.

I EDIT to avoid the judgments of others.

very busy BUSY

BUSY

I'm busy BUSY

BUSY

I'm very busy

I'm bus BUSY BUSY

BUSY busy very

I'm very

BUSY VERY BUSY VERY B

VERY BUSY

busy busy BUSY

Why are you so busy?
so busy?
so busy?

sy

Working, running around, always doing something.

Why?

To prove something?
To get something?
Avoiding life?
for self worth?

ery busy

isy

When I'm busy, I limit myself in my capacity to be me.

"I wish I had more time. 24 hours is just not enough time for me to do everthing I want to do.

Work is hectic right now – has been for the past 15 years. I really do want to spend more time with my family. I don't have much time for myself either. When I get my FU money then I'll slow down and enjoy life. Almost there."

Dad

How much of my life has been truly mine,
and not some agenda derived from his.

Our lives are like

old records.

Sometimes we hear

the same thing

over and over
over and over
over and over
over and over
over and over

over and over
over and over

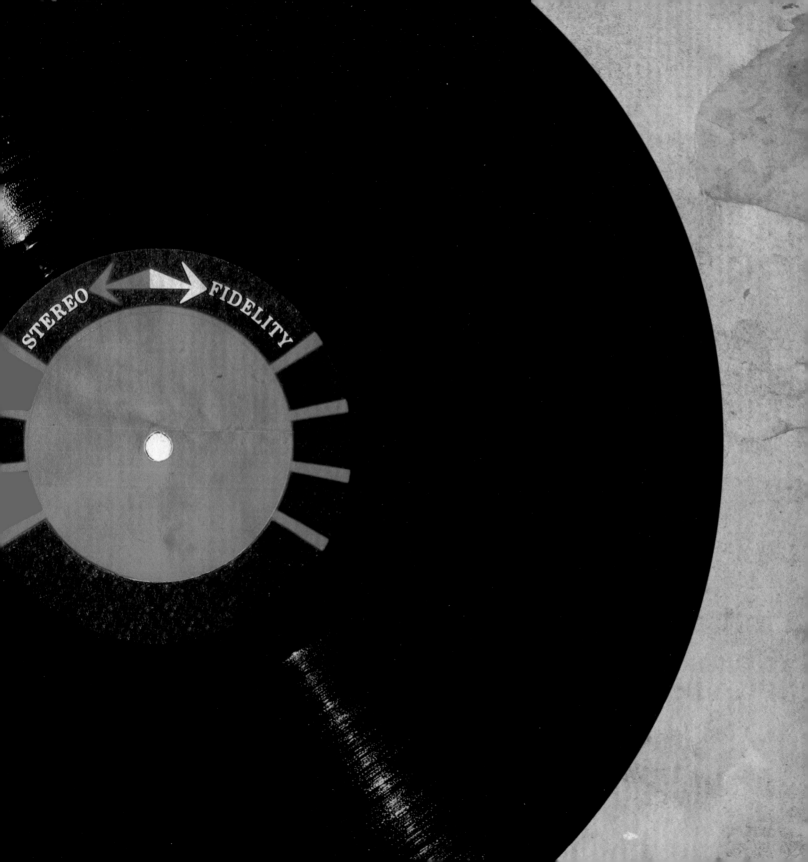

We can easily forgive a child
who is afraid of the dark.
The real tragedy of life
is when an adult
is afraid of the light.

Plato

SOUL QUESTIONS

Are you happy with your life?

Do you love what you're doing?

What part of your story is holding you back?

Sabotaging you?

What part of your story is a Gift?

How does your story serve you?

What truth about yourself is difficult to face?

What part of you
do you need to **reclaim?**

2

THE BOX

Layer 2
THE BOX

You are not your circumstances. You are not your beliefs. You are not your ego. You are not your flaws or your crutches.
You are not your perceptions or your stereotypes.

You are more than that. You are beyond that.

You are more powerful and full of life than you'll ever know.

Yet, like many people, you may not
fully tap into that essence.
You don't use your power,
you don't let it grow beyond your
invisible boundaries,
you don't live fully.

But why?

The truth is our story creates a box.

A box we live within. A box full of others' self-limitations.
A box full of routines and habits.
A box full of others' expectations.

The box is very familiar to you.

You, and the people and experiences around you, have created it.

It's your comfort zone. It's what you know.

Inside this box, **your life feels somehow shallow.** It feels like an act, like you're pretending, and it can leave you without fulfillment. For the most part, that feeling is true. You are not living your own life. Instead, you are living the life others want you to live, a life defined by the box.

You have become the persona you created to get love and approval from others, to protect yourself and help you navigate your life. **You are following the crowd.** Doing what you're supposed to do. **Staying in line.**

Dealing with obligations and responsibilities the way you were taught.

Jian works for his global family business.
He is a part of the fourth generation that has assumed responsibility for running the company.
He is married and has two beautiful children.
He has been in the family business for 15 years and is at a **key transition point.**
It is time for the third generation to hand over leadership of the business to the fourth generation. He is one of **the family members chosen to lead** the business for the next 10-15 years.

This new role would require him to uproot his life, his home and his family, and move overseas.

The problem is, Jian doesn't want to do it.

He doesn't want to move his family.
He doesn't want to run the family business.
He doesn't want to deal with the politics of managing family members across the globe. ▼

He gets miserable just thinking about it.

He is happy in his current position, home and lifestyle and frankly, **he doesn't need the money.** Yet, he was going to do it.

Jian was going to make a **life-altering decision** he had no interest in making.

He was going to change his whole life just to stay inside his box.

Like a drone, he was going to do only what he was programmed to do.

He was going to ignore, perhaps, what his own soul was telling him.

He was going to heed the words of his father, who told him **it was his responsibility** to run the family business.

He was going to "suck it up" and pretend to be happy, pretend to want what his father wants, pretend the family business drives his life.

After all, for years, it is the position his father had been **grooming him for.** It was his father's will.

Jian felt it was his **duty** to take a position he didn't really want.

He felt it was his **responsibility** to his father, and the family, to make a dramatic change he felt was wrong for himself and his family. **Duty** and **responsibility**

- these are the beliefs that have an invisible grip on his life and form the edges of his box.

It is what he learned works to get love and approval from his dad.

He doesn't want to disappoint his father or his family.

He has spent his whole life working and proving himself to win his father's approval and love.

His father loves him. His father just wants the best for his son.

But his father has an agenda he thinks is best for Jian.

He wants Jian to conform to the life he sees for him, a life that includes total dedication to the family business, as he had.

In truth, Jian has a lot to be thankful for. The family business has provided for his family through the years.

It has allowed him to live the lifestyle he has become accustomed to.

He is grateful for that and understands the opportunities he has been afforded.

Even if he chose to make this change, he would still be living a "good" life.

However, this is not about good versus bad. For Jian, his story has helped him find great success in his life.

It has served him well. But there is a point where the story becomes a double-edged sword.

There is a point where the story can serve or sabotage. Jian has reached that point.

No matter how much success you find
within the parameters of your story,
you are always limited. Your story can keep
you safely trapped inside the box. **It can limit your capabilities,**
breed complacency and keep
you from reaching your full potential.

Or your story can be your teacher.

It is important we know and recognize the difference.

It is important we **learn to make our story work for us,** instead of allowing it, and the people around us, to control the strings, as we become the puppet inside the box.
It's about managing your choices.
The choices you make create YOUR life. They are what makes your life unique to you.
Our stories influence these choices in such a way many times we are not even conscious
of the impact they have on us.

Stepping outside your story and becoming aware of how it influences
your life is the key to joy, happiness and fulfillment.

Jian has a life-changing choice in front of him. No matter what he decides, he must first recognize his own
story and the affect it has on him. He must see, clearly, the borders of the box he has been living in,
the box he has created because of the love he has for, and wants from, his father.
His story may teach him you don't have to do anything to be loved. You don't have to perform, achieve,
run the family business or be the perfect son.

Just be yourself.

If he finds that recognition, that awareness, then he will be able to make his own choice, find true
fulfillment, and live a life that is fully alive. ▶

Life goes on. Each day has a dronelike
quality to it. We follow the same routine.
the same routine. the same routine. Think
the same thoughts. the same thoughts. the
same thoughts...........

Stay inside the same box and tell
ourselves the same story.

Most of us are blind to it.

We ignore what our souls tell us to do.

I
PRETEND
TO
LIVE

i pretend to be happy
when i'm in pain.

Suffering.

i pretend to have friends
when i really feel alone.

i pretend to be in love.

i pretend that money, sex
and power fulfill me.

I WANT YOU TO FIT INTO MY BOX.

I WANT YOU TO CONFORM.
              TO HOW I SEE LIFE.
HOW YOU SHOULD BE.
  HOW YOU SHOULD ACT

HOW YOU SHOULD LOVE ME

  HOW YOU SHOULD ACCEPT ME.
HOW YOU SHOULD AGREE WITH ME.

I WANT YOU TO BE A COPY OF ME.
THIS IS MY EGO AT WORK.

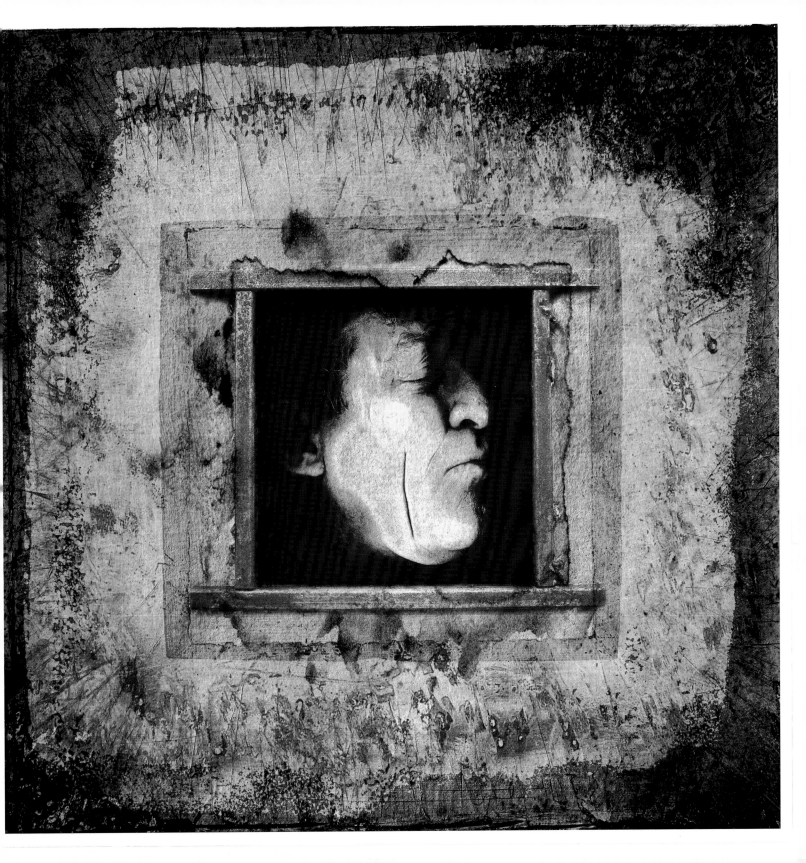

WORK

It's all I did.
It's all I thought about.
Work was my life.
I put it first before;
my family
my friends
me
before everything else.

I wanted money and power.
I wanted control.
I wanted to be seen as a success.
I used it to define me.
I worked my ass off.

I got money. I got power.
I got success. I was 'in control'.

Big deal.

I missed time with my wife.
I missed my kids growing up.
I missed enjoying the journey.

I lost sight of life.

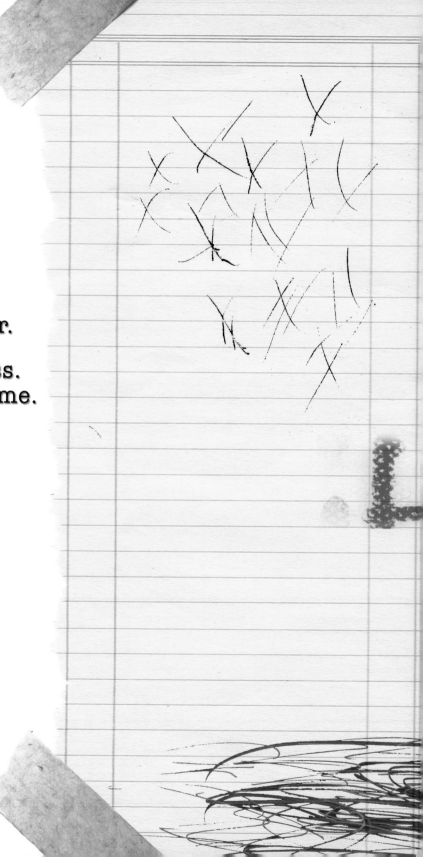

I have been leading a false life for so long
that I am not who I have been pretending to be.

The strings are connected to what others think of me.

To what others want me to be.

I dance to their tune.
I know how to do it very well.

It gets old.

When you come to a fork in the road - take it.

Yogi Berra

SOUL QUESTIONS

What are on the edges of your Box?

Are you afraid to step outside your Box? **What would happen?**

How does staying in your comfort zone serve you?

Where are you pretending in your life?

What habits and routines keep you stuck?

What do you do to keep pushing the edges of your box?

What is the **vision** you have for your life?

Layer

3 BLOCKS

Layer 3
BLOCKS

Fear. Limiting beliefs. Shadows. Blame. Judgment. Resentment.

They limit us.
They box us in.

We all have them.

They are the tools our ego uses to prevent us from moving outside of what we know.

They keep us trapped; keep us from **tapping into the full potential** of who we can become.

Fear. These are the mental monsters we create in our mind. It's a huge part of our conscious and unconscious thought. They tell us, **"you're not good enough, you're not smart enough, you're not worthy, you don't exist, you're not lovable..."**

Fear is insidious, permeates every part of our lives, and alters our decisions and actions on a daily basis.

It drains our energy, our passion and our ingenuity.

Fear attempts to control and protect us through its false and limiting messages. It is a master storyteller, telling us lies about ourselves and the world around us.

Limiting beliefs.
They hold us down and keep us small. They are one of our core filters through which we see and process the world around us. What you think, you will become. Beliefs like "a woman's place is in the home, good things happen to good people and bad things happen to bad people, money is the root of all evil, you have to look out for number one, nice guys finish last, you should be seen and not heard..." They are learned beliefs that become a part of our operating system.

If we allow them to operate unchecked, **they will limit our ability** to fully express who we are and sabotage us.

Blame.
We see ourselves as the victim. It's not my fault. It's their fault, they did it to me. It's the economy's fault. It's the government's fault. It's my partner's fault. It's my boss' fault. It's my parents' fault. We take the **spotlight** off ourselves and shift it to someone or something else. **When we blame we give our power away and allow ourselves to get stuck.**

Judgment.
We judge other people. We compare ourselves to others. We measure ourselves against them and often try to feel bigger and smarter by making them smaller and dumber.

By judging others, we are essentially judging ourselves.

Resentments.
It is anger we won't let go of. It is baggage from the past we choose to carry. It's negative energy that keeps us connected to the past. We keep it alive inside of us because it somehow serves us. Maybe it's your reminder of how you were hurt. Maybe it's your fuel to get revenge. **Maybe it's a way to feel sorry for yourself.** Maybe it's a way you stay disconnected from relationships. Resentments are toxic to our mind, body and soul.

These blocks limit you and hold you back from living **a fulfilling and joyful life.** They sabotage you and your relationships.

During a past retreat, I was working with a man named Guy whose father was a very successful businessman from France. When the Germans invaded France during World War II, he survived because his father had money which enabled the family to escape.

A friend of the family was not so fortunate. This friend did not have the monetary means to escape and was killed. Out of this tragedy grew a belief you needed money to survive. Guy learned from his father, **that money can not only further your life**, but also **prevent** you from being killed. ◼

That became Guy's story: **"You need money to survive. If you don't have it, you could die."**

This story was created to help protect Guy from the gruesome consequences his family experienced during the war. It was a powerful fear and belief for a young man looking to find his way in the world, and it became a core driver for his decisions and life choices.

From then on, Guy worked hard to create wealth so that he could survive. One problem. No matter how much money he made, his story continued to make him believe he **never had enough to fully protect him and his family.**

It became a double-edged sword.

On one side, **this belief helped Guy create a very successful business** and a meaningful amount of money.

On the other side, he could never stop working. He never felt safe. **He never felt he had enough.** No matter how painful it became, how much he sacrificed to get money, he had to keep going. The thought of not having money scared him to death.

Inside his story is a powerful gift, yet he couldn't see it was sabotaging his life.

Guy was letting his story run his life and didn't know it. **Fear was firmly in the drivers seat.**

I believe fear is the number one block that prevents many people from living a joyful, passionate, fulfilling life.

Fear of failure, fear of not being smart enough, fear of not being good enough, fear of rejection, fear of embarrassment, fear of judgment, fear of...(**FILL IN THE BLANK FOR YOU**).

Fear prevents you from accessing your gifts and talents, from living an authentic life.

Another man I worked with, Bill, lost his father in 1985. He had never visited his father's grave since. He was angry at his dad. **He was upset and resentful.** Earlier in his life, his father had betrayed his love. His dad was not faithful to his mother and eventually they divorced. Bill blamed him for the divorce and all the pain the family experienced as a result. **The blame lead to resentment.**

Bill carried this resentment with him for much of his adult life.

He looked like his father. So every morning when he woke up and looked at himself in the mirror, he didn't like what he saw. **Bill resented the face staring back at him.**

Over time, his resentment continued to grow. It shaped him. **It was like a steel cable that connected him to his past and he couldn't let go. It became his story.**

And it hindered him from living a life filled with joy and passion. Instead,

he was stuck living with rage and anguish.

Bill was sabotaging his life. All because he was pissed off at his father, **who was dead.**

Why do we fear? Why do we judge? **Why do we resent?** Why do we create a perception of limitations? **Why do we blame others** instead of looking inward?

The human psyche is complex,

and without understanding, it can be an endless and frustrating maze that leads us back to where we started. **So, we must take the time to understand the anatomy of our blocks.**

We must shine the light into the darkness.

When you **take the time and make the effort** to examine your blocks, you can learn how to redirect the negative and destructive power into one that can benefit your life. When you bring this negativity into the light of conscious awareness, **it will transform how you see yourself and the world around you.**

Guy was consumed by money. And because of it, he could not capture ultimate success. If Guy could see the essence of this energy was just trying to protect him and his family, it would reframe

how he works with the energy and transform his life.

Bill was handcuffed to his anger and resentment. Every day began and ended with rage at the man he saw in the mirror. Underneath all this negativity is Bills' gift of forgiveness.

Both of these mens' lives were dominated by the blocks in their stories and ultimately they were boxed in.

Once we have bought into the story of "who I am", we shut down the possibility of accessing the gifts and the full potential of who we can become.

If we do not take the time to **recognize and understand these blocks,** we are destined to remain trapped and lost. ▶

When is enough enough

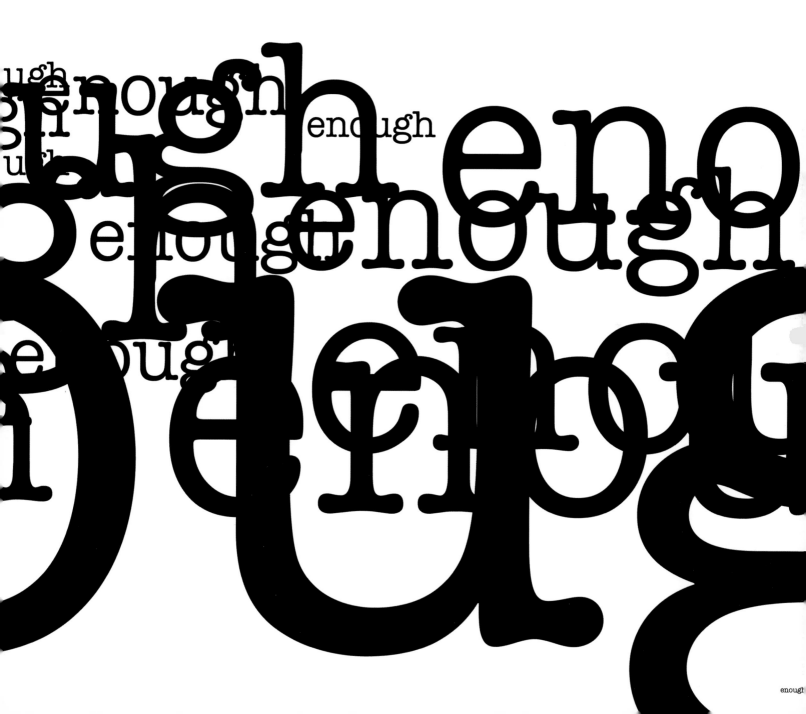

FEAR IS NOTHING MORE THAN A
MENTAL MONSTER YOU HAVE CREATED.

ALL YOUR FEARS ARE NOTHING MORE
THAN IMAGINARY GREMLINS.

Every time fear prevents you
from taking some action,
you have added fuel to its fire.
But when you conquer your fears,
you conquer your life.

Fear is a conditioned response;
a life-sucking habit that
can easily consume your energy,
creativity and spirit if
you are not careful.

Understand the anatomy of fear.
It is your own creation.
Like any other creation,
it is just as easy to tear it
down as it is to erect it.

Resentments are like a steel cable that keep us connected to our past.

what Resentments are
you holding on to?

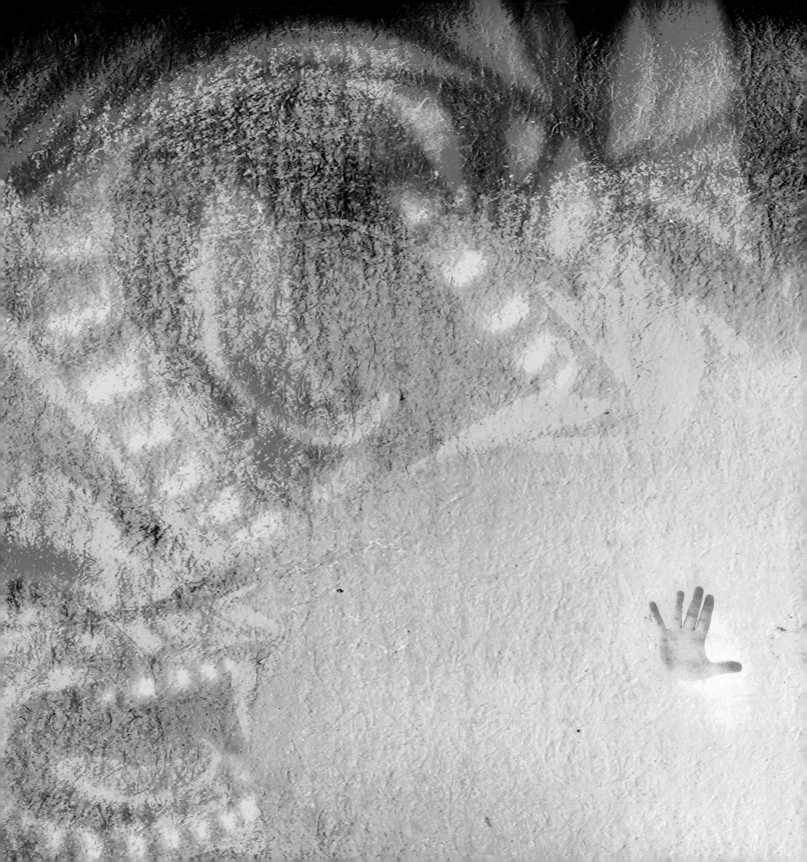

There are tiMes when I feel A l o n e

alone

I shUt dOWN   I feel DrAineD

I don't take cAre of myself

I disconnect   tired   I NumB

SpiRiTually   MYSELF

i fEEL lOsT

I tell myself that nobody cares

NOBODY

appreciates me

I CreaTe this PlaCe LoVes me

stUck Say

I isolate myself

WHY I LIE.

WHAT	WHY
I stole $ from my partner.	I deserve the money. I worked harder than him.
I cheated on my wife.	It's just sex and it's no big deal.
I cheated on my taxes.	I'm entitled to what I earn and I pay my fair share anyway.
I exaggerated and bullshitted still do.	To make myself look good and to be liked by others.
When I made mistakes I covered them up.	I'm afraid of failing. No one will ever know anyway.

I can rationalize why I lie.
I even make myself believe that I'm telling the truth.

Wow... what bullshit
I tell myself.

Lying is Lying.
No matter how I try and rationalize

TRUTH
At least for me it is.
Telling the truth is hard.

Tell the complete truth.
All the time.
All the time.
All the time.

Try it!

Behind all this,
some great happiness
is hiding.

Yehuda Amichai

SOUL QUESTIONS

What fears **hold you back** from living life fully?

What limiting beliefs keep you small?

To whom or what do you give your power?

What resentments do you hold?

What steel cable keeps you **connected to your past?**

How do these blocks sabotage **you?**

Who are you?
Why are you here?

STEP OUTSIDE YOUR STORY

073

PAIN

Layer 4
PAIN

Pain and suffering suck... or so I thought.

For most of my life, I did everything I could to avoid pain.
Why would anyone want pain and suffering to be part of their life?

Minimize pain and maximize pleasure. That was my goal.
It didn't work.

Pain is a part of life. It is unavoidable. As much as I tried to avoid it, I couldn't.
When I tried to push it away, it came back - sometimes even stronger than before.

So I decided to 'reframe' pain.

If pain was showing up in my life, there must be a reason for it. If I could find the reason for the pain,
or the healing behind it, then I could transform it and learn from it.

So my new goal was this: face the pain head on.
Get through it by understanding the "message" and the "healing" it offers.

Pain and suffering are a necessary and critical part of life.
Without pain and suffering, we would not be able to learn the lessons we are meant to learn
or heal the wounds of our past. I believe that everyone in my life, even those who cause me pain,
are there for a reason.

Pain is a messenger.
Knowledge, wisdom and healing are
hidden underneath it.

Once you are able to process your pain,
you will be able to achieve more happiness.

This thought process is far from the norm. Take a moment to think of your emotions like bandwidth. If you try to keep the bandwidth narrow - minimize the pain and suffering - then your happiness will be minimized too. If you allow the bandwidth to expand - work through the pain and suffering and process it fully - **then the bandwidth for happiness expands with it.**

The soul's primary purpose is to progress toward healing.

In that sense, pain is an important step toward healing. And since it is soul work, the pain will continue to return until you face it and learn to use it toward the soul's healing.

Anne was six years old when her father put her to work on the family farm. She began by helping with some of the simpler chores. As she got older, the work got both harder and longer. She would work every day after school and every weekend. Her father pushed her hard. He criticized her if she didn't do the job right. He verbally abused her.

He would yell, "If you were a boy, you'd be strong enough...you never do anything right...no man would ever want you...you're stupid... **you're a waste of my time."**

Anne wouldn't fight back. If she did, the abuse only got worse.

She learned to repress her anger and shame. She blocked out her emotions in order to survive. She buried her pain.

Her father's hurtful words had a deep and lasting impact on Anne.

She was an only child and her father wanted a son. He resented she was a girl.

Her mother would say to her, **"your father really loves you, he doesn't mean those things.** He's a good man and has a lot on his mind. He works hard to provide for us. Everything will be OK."

Everything was not OK.▫

Anne grew up emotionally numb, with low self-esteem, and had difficulty in relationships with men. After she left home, she spent the rest of her life trying to prove she was good enough, that she was worth the time. This became her story.

I met Anne when she was 42-years-old. She was the CEO of her own company. She never married. **In the eyes of most, she was a tough woman - successful and able to keep up with the men.**

But underneath her tough exterior, she was in pain. She was lonely, sad and unhappy. She was suffering and wanted a way out.

What Anne did not realize, is the **answer is not out, but down and in.** Anne needed to **go into the pain** to learn what it had to teach her. Getting the message and healing by going into the pain is also the way through it.

At its root, Anne's pain was caused by her feelings of inadequacy. She wasn't good enough to be wanted or loved. She was holding on to her anger and resentment. Holding on to this negative energy only hurt Anne. It was a poison eating at her from the inside.

She would move in and out of relationships with men. They would leave her because she was cold and emotionless. She had difficulty accessing and expressing her emotions which led to a lack of intimacy. **Or worse, she would attract verbally abusive men.**

She was repeating a pattern she learned from her father. Growing up, she learned to stuff her emotions

and put up with abuse in order to be safe.

But her pain was teaching her this pattern didn't work anymore. At 42 years of age, it was time to heal the wound of her past and transform the pain.

By listening to her pain, she learned she was good enough just as she is and her emotions are powerful enough to help her connect to herself and to others. She learned to access those emotions and let them flow.

In turn, her pain gave her incredible strength and the ability to **stand strong in tough situations.**
She learned to see the gift and the message in the pain and transform it.

Going deep into difficult wounds is hard.

A friend of mine, Mary, had a son, Michael, with a mental illness. She blamed herself. It was her fault her son was autistic. She held on tight to her guilt, and felt she was a bad mother because she couldn't fix the situation. But she had to keep trying. If she gave up, she simply couldn't live with the guilt.

Holding on to this guilt was squeezing the life out of her.
She stopped taking care of herself. She gained 80 lbs and was depressed most of the time.
It affected her relationships with her husband and two children.

Her pain overshadowed all the beauty in her life.

Her pain was running her life. Many of us learn how to cope with our pain.
We find ways to feel better, to separate ourselves from the pain. We distract ourselves from dealing with the real issue.

As difficult as it may be, **Mary needed to go deep in to her wound and learn to cope with her guilt.**
She needed to learn how to decipher the message this emotion had for her.

Until Mary, or any of us, learns to decipher that message, the pain will remain buried inside us.
We have to be willing to examine the baggage - all of it - and drag it out, no matter how nasty, smelly or embarrassing it is.

What pain are you avoiding?

Ask yourself that question. And as you begin to transform the pain in your life,
you will access more of your own joy and happiness. ▶

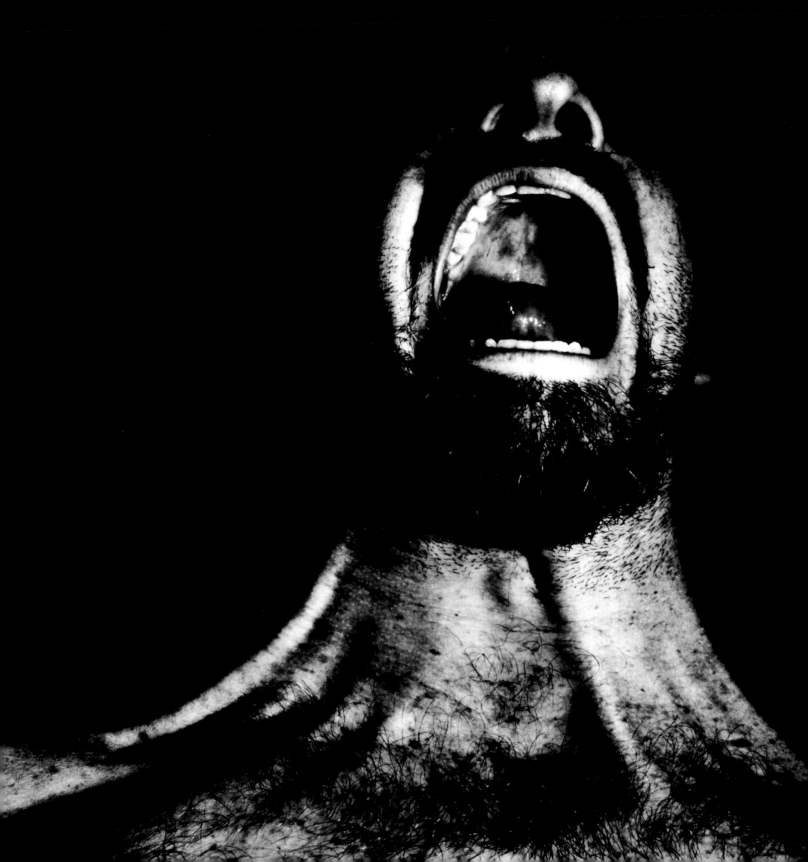

HAVE YOU EVER FELT SO MUCH PAIN
THAT YOUR SOUL SCREAMED OUT LOUD

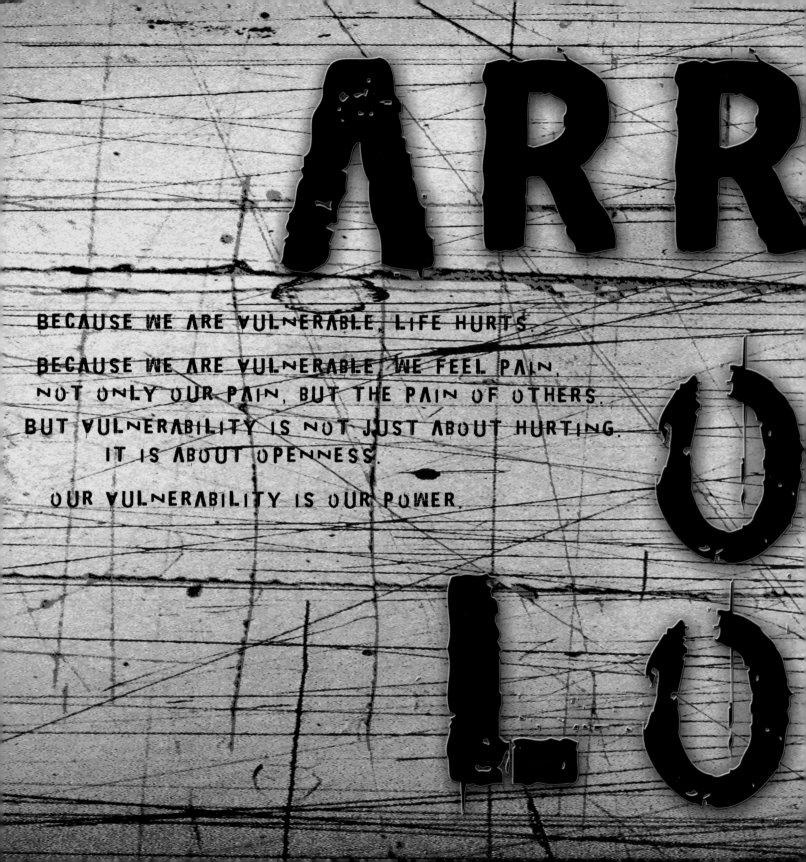

BECAUSE WE ARE VULNERABLE, LIFE HURTS.

BECAUSE WE ARE VULNERABLE, WE FEEL PAIN,
NOT ONLY OUR PAIN, BUT THE PAIN OF OTHERS.
BUT VULNERABILITY IS NOT JUST ABOUT HURTING,
IT IS ABOUT OPENNESS.

OUR VULNERABILITY IS OUR POWER.

Going further into Despair,
   grants us access to HOPE.

Going fully into Pain,
   grants us access to HEALING.

Going fully into the Dark,
   opens us to the LIGHT.

take it anymore

YOU

dumb shit

fucking lying piece of shit

JERK

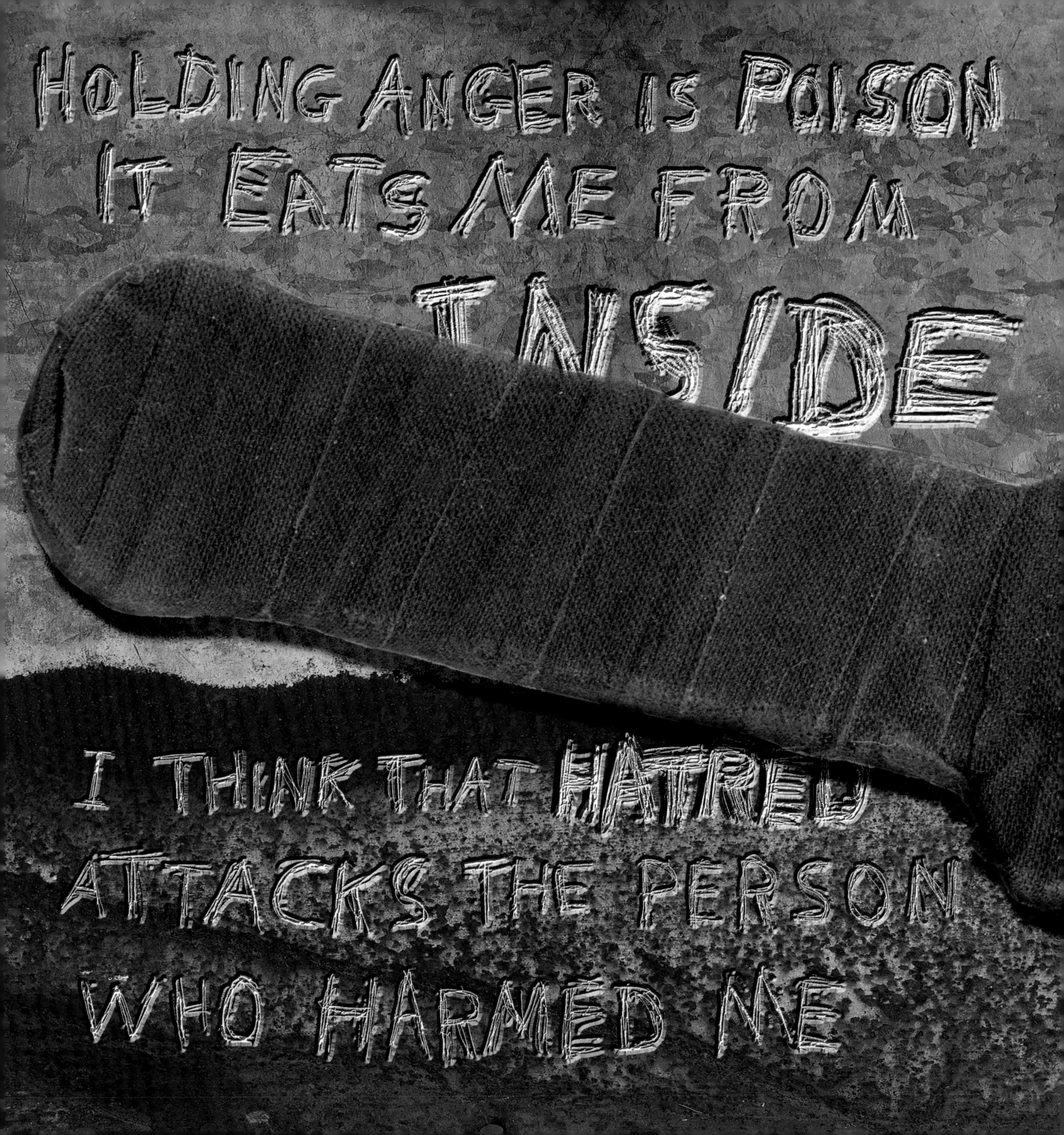

Holding Anger is Poison
It Eats Me from
INSIDE

I Think that HATRED
ATTACKS THE PERSON
WHO HARMED ME

BUT HATRED IS A CURVED BLADE

THE HARM I DO
I DO TO MYSELF

WE Hold tight onto our MOney.
We holD Tight Onto ouR ReLationshipS.
We HOld tight onTo our STuFF.
We Hold TiGht onto Our BeliEfs.

When we hold on so tight, it creates pain that overshadows the beauty.

The man who fears suffering is already suffering from what he fears.

Michel De Montaigne

SOUL QUESTIONS

What is the gift of the pain in your life?

What do you do to minimize or avoid pain?

What is the message in your most recent painful experience?

What needs to be healed?

What baggage needs to be examined?

What beliefs are you holding onto that limit you?

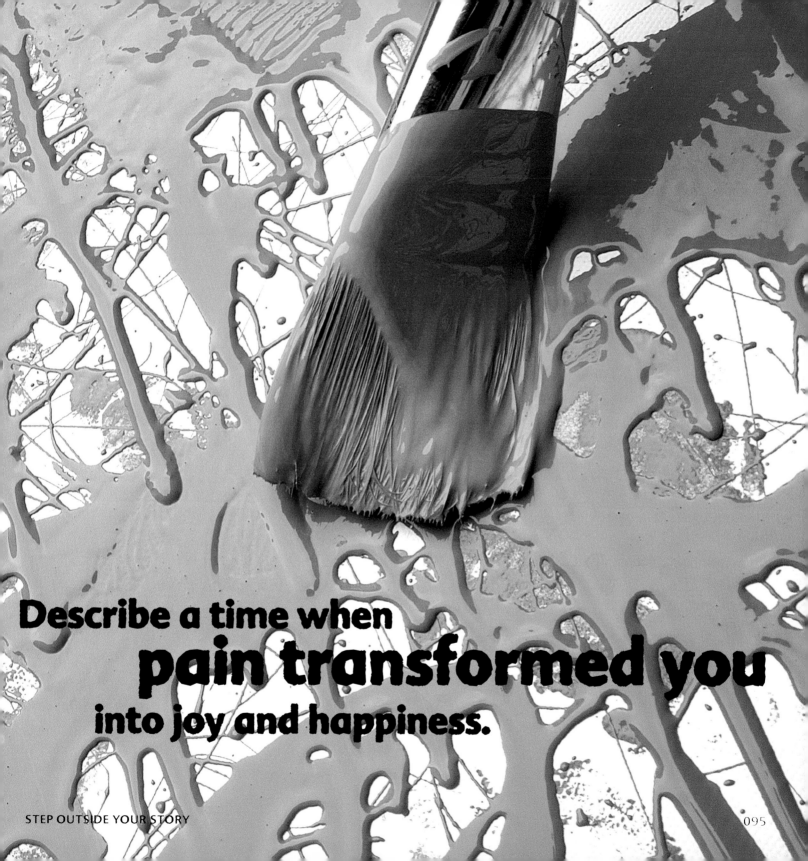

Describe a time when **pain transformed you** into joy and happiness.

Layer

Layer 5
LIVE BY

Life is hard. Life is not fair. Life is unpredictable. Life hurts.

Most people work extremely hard to avoid pain, hardship and suffering.
But the fact remains: life is difficult and many times,
most of the time, pain is unavoidable.

Life simply does not always act the way we want it to.
It doesn't always respond to our specific wants and desires, doesn't fit neatly in
to the little box that represents our expectations.
Then again, if life were easy,
it would lose its purpose.
If life were easy, it would lose much of its fulfillment. It is in overcoming
hurdles and facing challenges that we find life's true value.
Overcoming is what feeds our soul with virtue and purpose.

So instead of working to avoid the pain and the suffering, we should instead focus on awareness.

Acknowledge that all life includes pain, and prepare for it.
Once we are prepared, we can face it and go through it.

Prepare to face the pain. And be aware that things change and die.

Things change all the time. Nothing is static or fixed. Nothing is guaranteed.
Anything can change, anything can die, anything
can end, everything is impermanent.
Yet, most people have an aversion to this truth. People can't envision things ending or changing.
We seek security and comfort and hold onto the idea of avoiding change. We reject it.
We try to control the uncontrollable. We try to dictate the terms of our life.
This resistance is what causes our suffering.

We resist, instead of realizing when something ends, something new also begins.

We resist, instead of finding opportunity in the ever-changing landscape of our lives.

We resist, even though one door closing, means another door is opening.

Life is unpredictable.

We never know what is going to happen next. The next moment could be the last.

Life could be over, in an instant.

But that makes it real. That makes us mortal and limited.

So why not be willing to take risks? Why not revel in life's mystery, give in to its magic?

We don't realize it, but uncertainty is important. We naturally want things to be predictable.

We want to avoid trouble, instead of facing it. We want to know what we are facing.

But this is impossible, so why fight it?

Why not accept it? Why not accept that in not knowing, we take part in a journey of self-discovery, a journey toward knowledge and recognition, a journey that is essential to living a life that is fully alive.

Unpredictability is an undeniable part of life. But it can work for us.

We can take the unexpected suffering and turn it into learning.

This uncertainty should be precious to us,

because we can use it, it can help us grow.

Suffering can be a wake up call.

It can be a slap in the face to wake us up and send us moving in the right direction. No, pain is not the enemy.

Pain is a gift just waiting to be harnessed,

waiting to help, waiting to give us more insight into ourselves. ▼

It doesn't mean you should be looking for pain.

But if pain is chasing you, turn and face it.

Accept its message, analyze it, process it, understand it, and move through it.

Much of our suffering comes because we resist the natural course of life.

When we resist what life brings us, when we resist dealing with the truth of our reality, when we deny, repress and avoid life's challenges, suffering kicks in.

Suffering can be a great teacher.

It can show us what needs to change or what needs more attention.

Depression, physical pain, low self-esteem, relationship troubles – all these things cause suffering and demand our attention. But those things also act as signposts in life's long, winding journey.

Suffering is a power guidance system for us.

Suffering creates awareness for things that aren't working, things you're resisting, things that need to be addressed or focused on.

We should be thankful for this. As much as we don't want to admit it, we need those signs. We are not as aware as we think we are.

Simply put, we are not in control.

The only thing we truly have total control of in our life is our choices.

That's it. Only choice. If you believe you can control anything else, you are delusional. Guess what? **Most of us are delusional. Me included.**

But what you don't realize, is that feeling of powerlessness, of not being in control, can be the ultimate gift. Only those who have felt truly powerless can feel true power. That's where the real spiritual journey begins.

When we feel as if we have power over nothing, that's when we are prepared to have power over our life and our choices.

But most believe they are still in **control.**

They believe they have all the **power.**

They believe that life should move and **bend to their will.**

They believe that's how it's always been, they have always been in **control.**

They don't realize
we are not that important.

We take ourselves so seriously that, in our minds, we make ourselves important.

We believe we are the center of the universe,
that life is all about us.

That's because in our minds, we are the center of the universe.

In our mind, our ego takes over. **Our ego wants to make itself important.**

It works overtime convincing us to be important, to be special, to be on top, to be the best, to be No. 1, etc.

The ego's job is to get approval and attention, to make it's owner feel important.

And without recognition or awareness, the ego always succeeds.

Unfortunately, that importance is not real.

It is the product of our ego, and the control it has over us.

We must break free of our ego. We must realize we are not that important.

We are not the center of the universe.

We are just part of a larger whole, and we must earn our way through this

journey by learning from our suffering, adapting to our pain, living with unpredictability,

and continuing to move forward nonetheless.

Many things in our life are out of our hands.
But we will always have our choices.

Life is hard. Life changes. Life causes suffering. Life is unpredictable. Life sometimes seems out of control.

We can choose to be overcome by this. Or we can accept the challenge, take the journey head on,

and choose to overcome it ourselves.

What is your choice? ▸

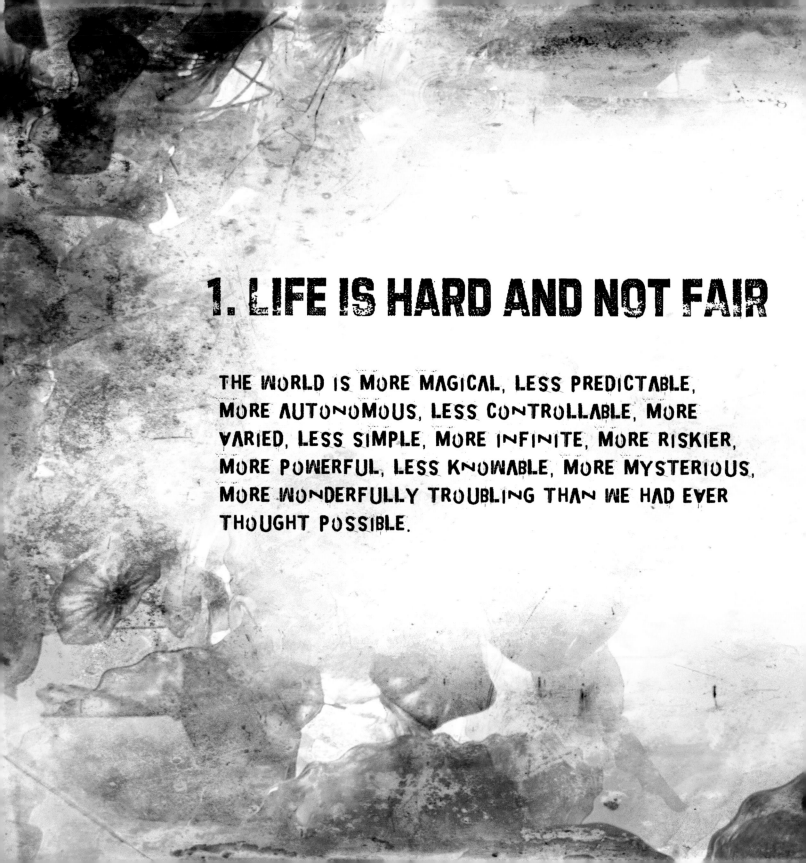

1. LIFE IS HARD AND NOT FAIR

THE WORLD IS MORE MAGICAL, LESS PREDICTABLE,
MORE AUTONOMOUS, LESS CONTROLLABLE, MORE
VARIED, LESS SIMPLE, MORE INFINITE, MORE RISKIER,
MORE POWERFUL, LESS KNOWABLE, MORE MYSTERIOUS,
MORE WONDERFULLY TROUBLING THAN WE HAD EVER
THOUGHT POSSIBLE.

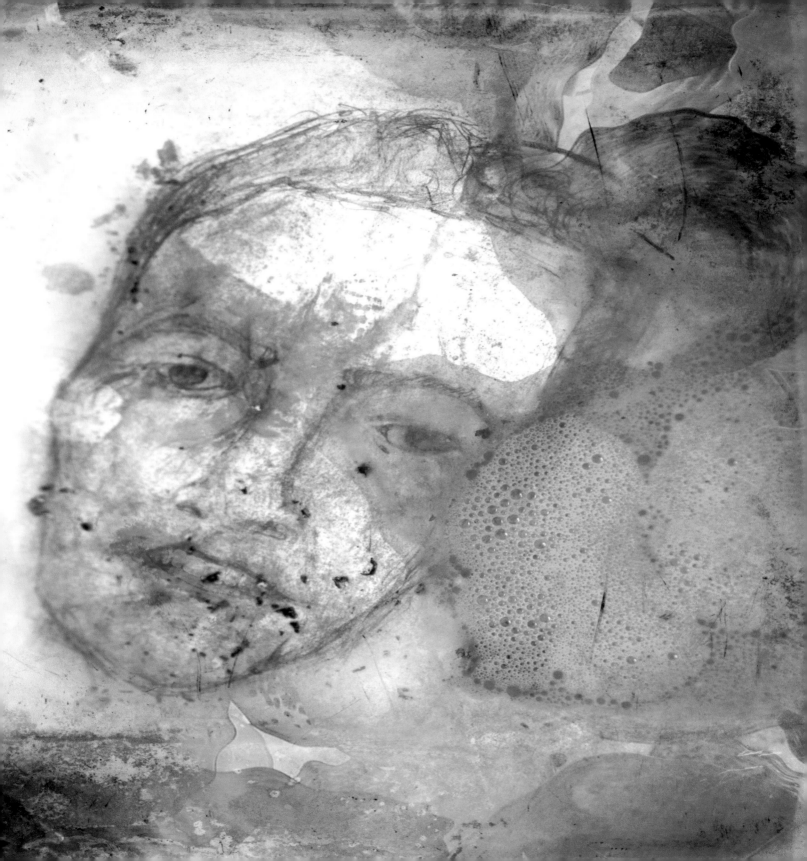

2. THINGS CHANGE AND DIE

The mortality and impermanence of our lives must become very real to us. Life here is limited and everything that happens to us is a school for death. Everything is passing away.

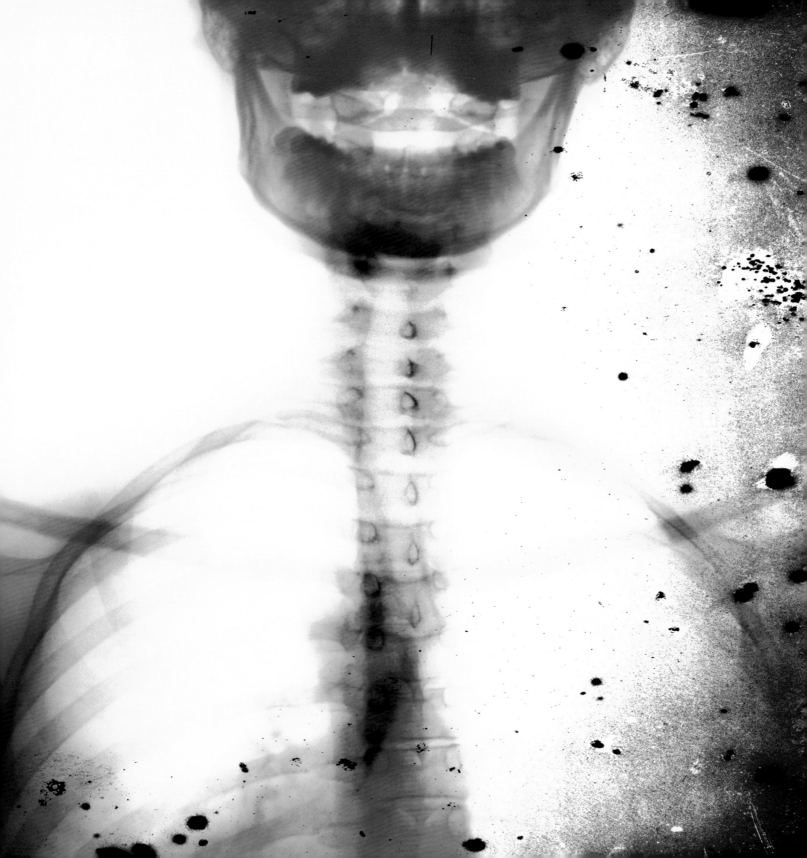

3. THINGS HAPPEN IN AN UNPREDICTABLE WAY

We can try to control the uncontrollable by looking for security and predictability, always hoping to be comfortable and safe. But the truth is that we can never avoid uncertainty.

4. SUFFERING IS A PART OF LIFE

Resisting life causes suffering. The root of this suffering is resisting the certainty that no matter what the circumstances, uncertainty is all we truly have.

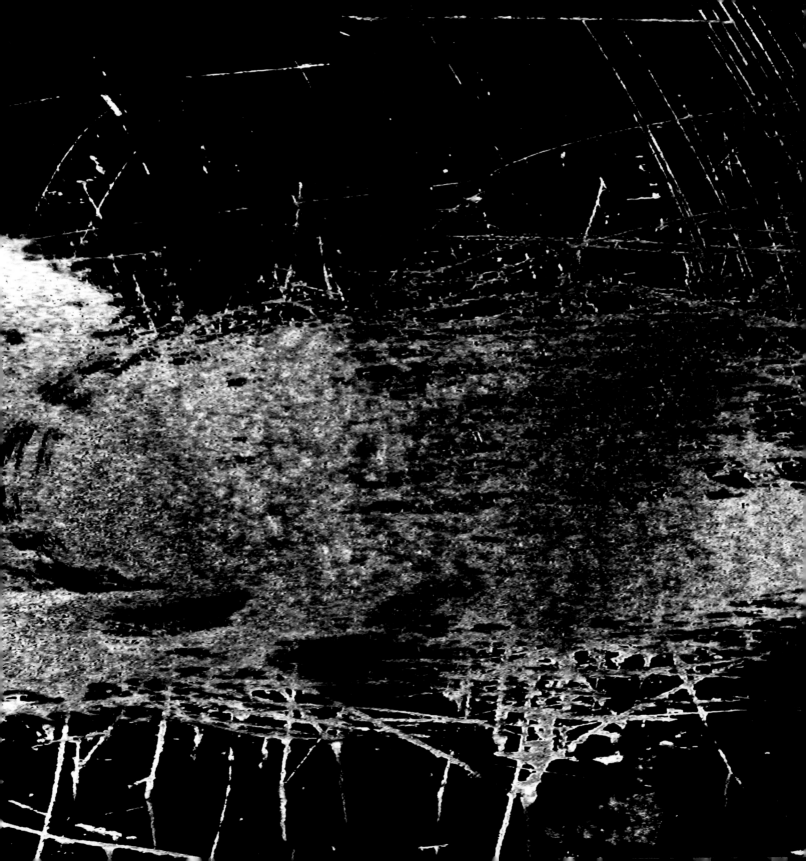

We live with the illusion that we
are in control. We must experience
our own powerlessness before a true
spiritual journey can begin.

5. YOU ARE NOT IN CONTROL

6. YOU ARE NOT THAT IMPORTANT

That we take ourselves so seriously, that we are
so absurdly important in our own minds, is a problem.
Self-importance is like a prison for us, limiting
us to the world of our likes and dislikes. We end
up bored to death with ourselves and our world.

"No man is free
who is not a master
of himself"

Epictetus

SOUL QUESTIONS

What part of your life is hard?

What hurts?

What pain are you
trying to avoid or deny?

What are you uncertain about?

What are you resisting that may be causing suffering?

What part of your life do you
need to let go of or change?

What part of your life feels unfair?

Layer

6 CHANGE

Layer 6 CHANGE

Your life is in your hands.
You have the power of choice.

You can always choose to change your circumstances.

You can decide to make things different or make things better. And yet, so many people resist change.

Why do they fight it?

Why do they make it so difficult when they have the ability to make things better?

Perhaps **they don't understand the effects of change** - that they can be deep and lasting. Perhaps they are worried change can be hard and can take time.

Indeed it can. But it can also be simple and instantaneous.

On September 1, 2005 I walked into Mike Maroone's office at 10 a.m., I stood in front of one of the most ambitious and successful men in the automotive industry, a man who had helped me build a thriving career for myself, and **I told him I was leaving AutoNation.**

I had been with the South Florida-based organization for almost nine years. **I had put a lot in to my job** there, had helped build the organization into one of the largest and most successful automotive retailers in North America.

But I had made a decision.
It was time to leave and follow my true passion.

The change was instantaneous.

It took one sentence: "Mike, I'm leaving AutoNation to do something different in my life."

Three seconds and it was done.

I felt my world change in those three seconds.

I felt lighter, elated, **silly, energized...**

and scared shitless.

120

Or the change can be hard, and take time.

On October 15, 2003, **I knew exactly what I wanted to do. I had a new vision for my life.**
I wanted to go in a new direction that centered on helping others create a life that is more fully alive.
I discovered a special gift I possess,
which I could use to help others manifest this change.
Once I had the clarity about my new direction, **the next step was to actually do it.**

Easy to say - hard for me to do.

The voices in my head

started to question this new direction. They started to create doubt.

These voices said, **"You can't do this.** You've never done anything
like this before. You can't make money at this.
You're going to leave a job that is paying you over $400,000 a
year with stock options to do this? Are you out of your fucking mind?
You have obligations. You have responsibilities.
You're going to throw away a 26-year career to do this?
You dumb shit. You are at the peak of your career.
You've worked so hard to get here. Don't give this up. What if you fail?

Don't do it!"

On and on and on.
These voices worked on me every day.
They wore me down. Muddied my vision. Diverted my thoughts.
Made it difficult to focus on making the decision to follow my heart, my passion.

The decision to change can be painfully hard, and it can take time.
It can take forever, especially if I listen to those voices
and let them run my life and make my choice for me.
I would never be able to make a change.

If I let them run the show I would never have made the decision to leave.◄

It took me two years to push through those fears before I had the courage
to go into Mike's office and give him the three-second
choice that I had finally made - two frigging years.

Now, I believe any choice of this size and scope **should be properly thought out, and planned,**
so a transition can take place in a healthy and responsible way.
I believe strongly in using your head in service to your heart.
But if it is fear that is holding me back, then I am wasting precious time and energy.

Taking two years to just make a decision was allowing my heart to be in service to my head.
All those voices were in my head. My heart, which was a much softer voice, said,
"Do it - you know it's what you are here to do. So just do it. Now."

If you want to change your life, **you first have to get a vision of your future,**
and a clear direction for where you want to go and why.
Before I made the change to leave my marketing career behind me,
**I had to create a new vision for my life and
get clarity on why I'm here
and my life's purpose.**
That clarity helped me navigate my decisions.
It helped me know what to say "yes" to and what to say "no" to.

Over the years, as I've done multiple retreats with the same groups, I've noticed the issues we talked
about in our first retreat are the same the next year, and again the next year.
I call these **groundhog issues** - after the movie Groundhog Day.
These issues are there every day
when you wake up,
and they are the same every single day.

We all have issues like this. We avoid dealing with them because
they are too difficult to address, the consequences are uncertain or **too terrifying** to even think about.

**So they just sit there,
ignored, yet begging to be addressed.**

As I see it, you have two ways you can address these groundhog issues.
You can proactively deal with them,
and cut them off before they turn into something even more painful.

Or you can wait for the train wreck.

Wait for some extremely destructive or significant emotional event which will force you to deal with them at a time when you may or may not be prepared to do so.

One way or another, you will deal with them.

A friend of mine, Jack, has been married to Carrie for 18 years and has two beautiful daughters. Katie is eight years old and Elizabeth is six. Jack says he's bored with the marriage. There is **no more intimacy, romance or sex in his partnership.** All of Carrie's time is focused on their children and there is no time for the marriage. He feels as if he and Carrie have drifted apart and lost the connection that made them fall in love and get married in the first place. They are more like **roommates** now instead of lovers. Yet, he is staying with her because of the kids. **He doesn't want to leave and hurt the kids.**

But Jack is seeing another woman. He tells the other woman he loves her and is going to leave his wife. Jack has been telling her this for over two years now.

This is a train wreck waiting to happen.

Jack has a choice. **He can be proactive** and deal with his difficult situation in a direct, loving and healthy way, a way that will be better for everyone, not just himself. Or he can wait for the train wreck to force something to happen.

I see hundreds of situations like this. People who are in **jobs they hate.** People who are in **relationships that don't work.** People who know they need to take better care of themselves, but don't. People who have **addictions they rationalize.** People who are **living in places they hate.** People who are unhappy, but won't make the necessary changes.

Most of us have a hard time dealing with change. **Change is scary, uncertain and unpredictable.** So we would rather keep the status quo instead of dealing with the consequences of change. **We think we can control the outcome** by managing the issue. Most of the time, this doesn't work. In fact, trying to control the issues, instead of fixing them or addressing them head on, can make them worse.

Change is a very real part of life. Change is where growth and learning comes from.
Change helps us move our lives forward. Change helps us open new doors. **Change helps us feel alive.**

Don't fear change. Find it. **Welcome it..**

INSTRUCTIONS:
APPLY AGRESSIVELY AND FIRMLY TO FOREHEAD
WHENEVER YOU REQUIRE MEANINGFUL CHANGE.

2X4

falling is easy
getting back up
becomes the problem

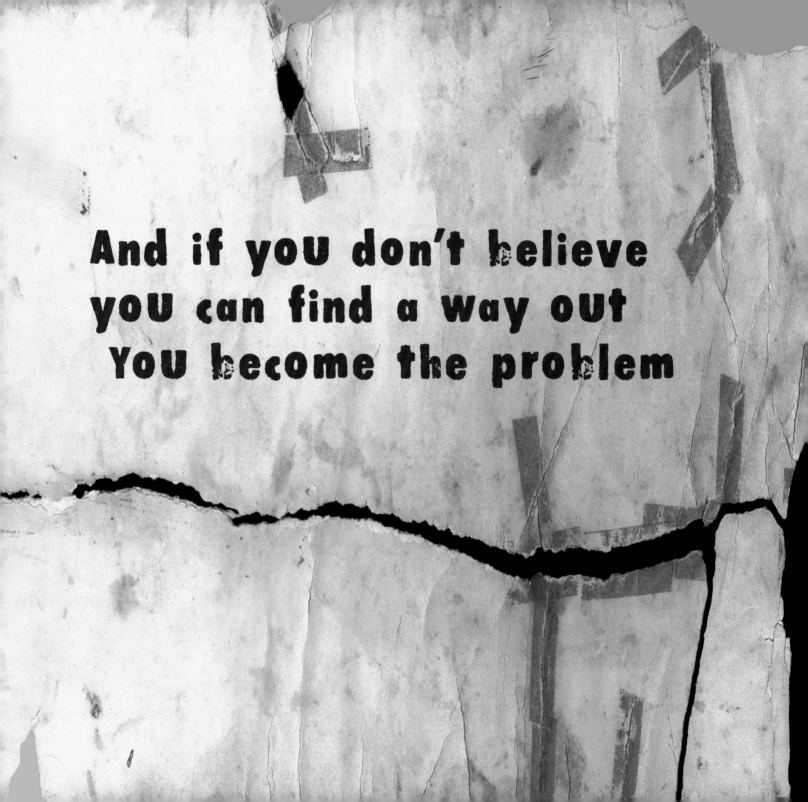

In our brokenness
is the source of
our light.

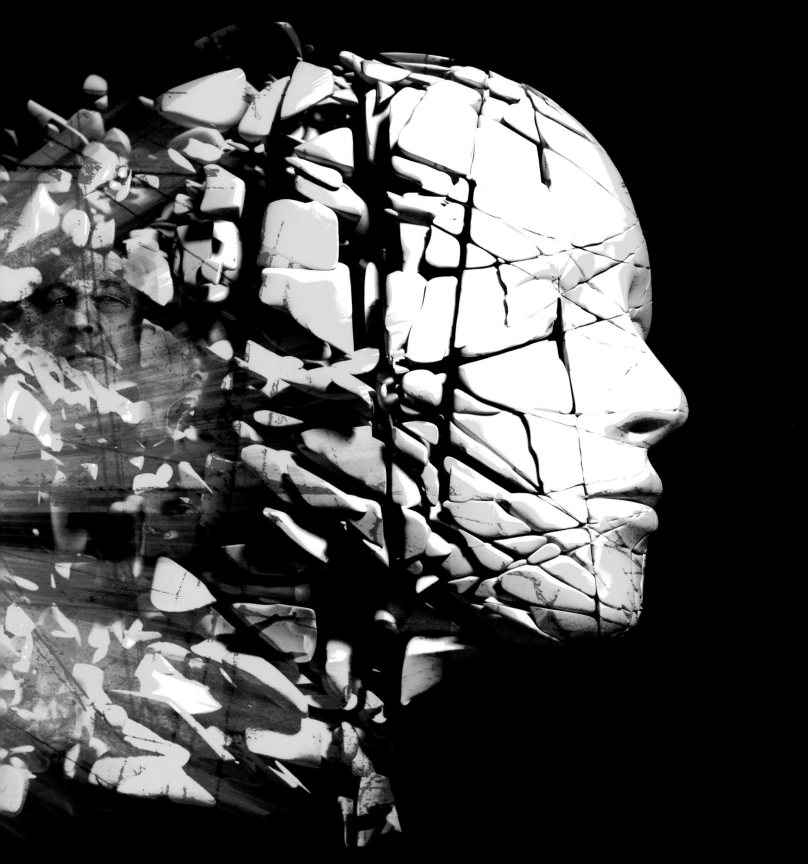

I walk, down the street.
There is a deep hole in the sidewalk.
I fall in.
I am lost....I am helpless.
It isn't my fault.
It takes forever to find a way out.

I walk down the same street.
There is a deep hole in the sidewalk.
I pretend I don't see it.
I fall in again.
I can't believe I am in the same place.
But it isn't my fault.
It still takes a long time to get out.

I walk down the same street.
There is a deep hole in the sidewalk.
I see it there.
I still fall in...it's a habit.
My eyes are wide open.
I know where I am.
It is my fault.
I get out immediately.

I walk down the same street.
There is a deep hole in the sidewalk.
I walk around it.

I walk down another street.

What is to give light
must endure burning.

Victor Frankl

SOUL QUESTIONS

What change are you resisting?

What is your groundhog issue?

How long has it been there?

Are you setting yourself up for a train wreck?

What fear blocks you from change?

What does the doubting voice in your head say to you about change?

Does your heart or head take the lead in your decisions?

What is one change that would **meaningfully impact** your life one year from now?

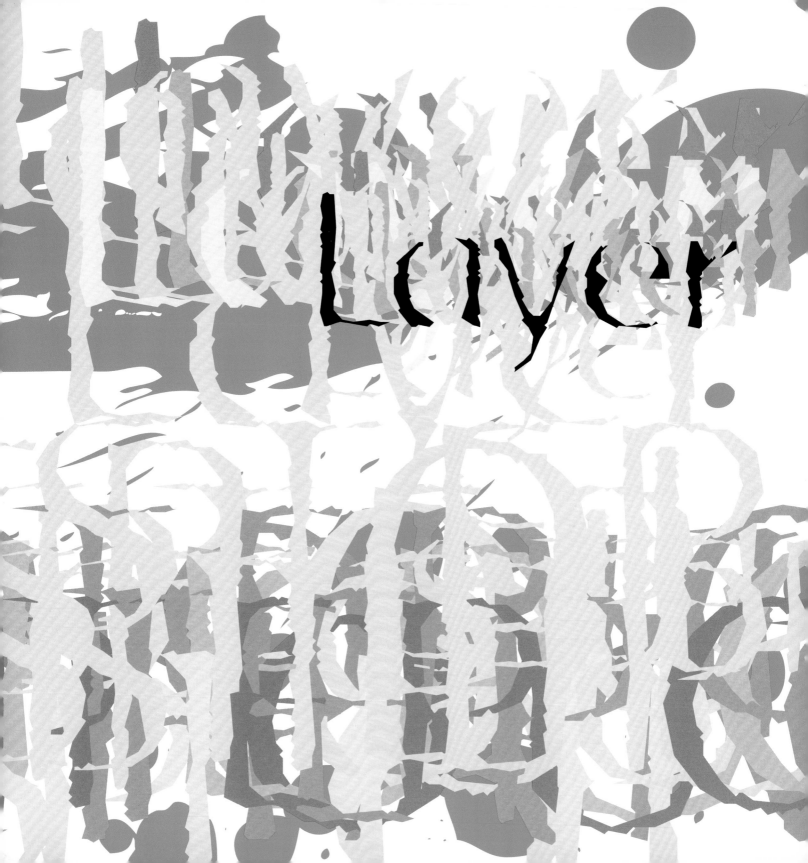

Layer

7 STEP OUTSIDE

Layer 7
STEP OUTSIDE

Our lives are the sum of our past choices.

At this very moment, we are encountering and experiencing things that are directly connected to the decisions and actions we have made that led up to this moment. **The past creates the consequences of the present. Yesterday helps craft today.**

A minute ago can affect a minute from now.

So if we're not happy with our current life,

if we're not doing what we enjoy doing, if we're not in loving relationships, we have only ourselves, and our own conscious decisions, to examine. If we are discontent in our life, it's time to make some different choices, some new decisions.

It's time to change.
It's time to realize we have the power
to create the life we want.

What we do with our life is up to us.

We are all on a journey of discovery.

The journey is challenging and full of opportunity.

And a significant part of that journey includes stepping outside our story to examine the life we are leading. As has been discussed, looking at our lives from an unbiased, third person perspective can open our eyes to some of the things we overlook when, in essence, they are right in front of us.

Stepping outside our story can help us learn about the unique recipe that brought us here, and how it supports and relates to our journey. It can **help us understand** the lens through which we see the world. It can **help us reclaim** the things that have been buried, denied or repressed. It can **help us learn how to identify and manifest our unique gifts in the world, and live a life of passion.**

On the other side of that coin, staying inside our story, and effectively **being blinded** by it, will only **limit the experience** of our life. Getting **stuck inside** our story, and **bound by a narrow** predetermined view of life, can **hold us back** from making new decisions, new choices, and experiencing all that our lives have to offer.

And what our lives have to offer is significant.

Sure, our story can attempt to keep us safe and comfortable. It tries to help us avoid pain and suffering. But it is also limiting. It can sabotage us from attaining fulfillment and feeling fully alive.

We are not here to lead an average, limited life.

In order for you to step outside your story you have to push on the edges of your comfort zone. Stepping outside will be uncomfortable. It will be difficult and even painful. **It will be like stirring a hornet's nest.** There's no denying that. But if you prepare for it, and you focus on the fruits of the end goal, **it will be a worthwhile journey.**

Any time you decide to push on the edges of your story, your inner voices will start to work overtime to keep you in line.

They will work, subconsciously, to protect you, to bind you, to comfort you, to keep you safe. ▼

Managing the intensity and virtual insanity
of that internal chatter can be a challenge.

The further you step outside the box and into the so-called unknown,

the louder and more aggressive

the internal chatter will get. It will tell you to **get back** into your comfort zone.

It will tell you to fall back to your old, safe, familiar patterns.

It will tell you to get back inside, before it's too late.

Get back into your story, or the pain will continue.

Analyzing our story has its place. As we've discussed, it can be useful to look at our story from every conceivable angle.

But it's no substitute for experiencing, for living in the present
and having a clear vision of our future.
The problem with looking at and analyzing

our past is that we can easily get caught up in it. **We can get stuck in our past.**

We only want to examine the past in order to **give us essential information** about what needs to change

in our life and **how we can use it** to live a life that is more fully alive.

To put it bluntly, **it's all about our choices** - how we choose to deal with our experiences,

our emotions, our relationships and ourselves. Reactively or proactively.

There is much to discover about being human, about living our lives.

The simple fact is, the more we know, the better equipped we are to make proactive choices
and decisions which help us build the lives we want.

I believe strongly that by working on our story, we release those parts of us that

prevent access to our joy and our true happiness. ## So by bringing awareness
to these blocks you will inevitably
access more of your true self,

and the changes you experience will be obvious and enjoyable.

As part of your journey, you will learn how to forgive yourself and others.

Forgiveness is a powerful process,

and it is one of the things that can block access to your true self.

It is a way of coming to grips with past choices, experiences and mistakes.

Along those same lines, being able to
live with a sense of gratitude and appreciation
can shift how you live each and every day. Are you grateful for what you have?
Or do you take for granted those things that surround you? Do you **appreciate**
what you've earned or achieved in life? Or do you strive, or think more about, what you don't have?
Are you afraid of losing what you have?

Stop. Hit "pause." Take time to reflect,
to pay attention to your life. To appreciate
what you already have,
who you love and who you are.

Plan to pause.

It's been said that in the instant before we die,
our life flashes before our eyes. If, in that moment, we are given a chance to take a look
back and see what we did with our lives, will we see a blessed and fulfilled soul,
rich with experiences and accomplishments we personally crafted and cultivated?
In short, would we be satisfied?

Are we living each day as though it might be our last?
Because the reality is that it could very well be our last.
If today was your last day and you looked back on your life, what would you say about it?

My hope for you is that you would say,
"WOW that was the most incredible experience ever! I lived my life full of passion, joy and love."

Enjoy the Journey of Discovery and live a life that is fully alive!

Passion Rules. ▸

Our destiny
is to bring
more
and more
consciousness
to
what is
now
unconscious.

complexity

simplicity

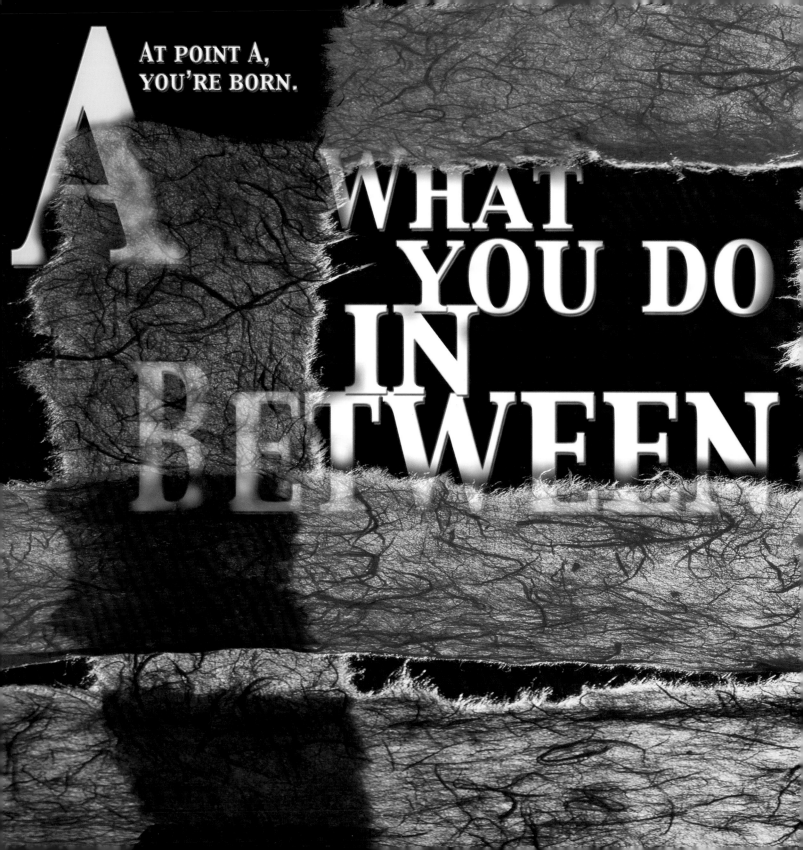

A AT POINT A, YOU'RE BORN.

WHAT YOU DO IN BETWEEN

IS UP
TO
YOU

At Point B, You're history.

Forgiveness has to come from inside as a desire of the heart.

Forgiving is about healing wounds.

We forgive when we feel a strong wish to be free from the pain that glues us to a bruised moment of the past.

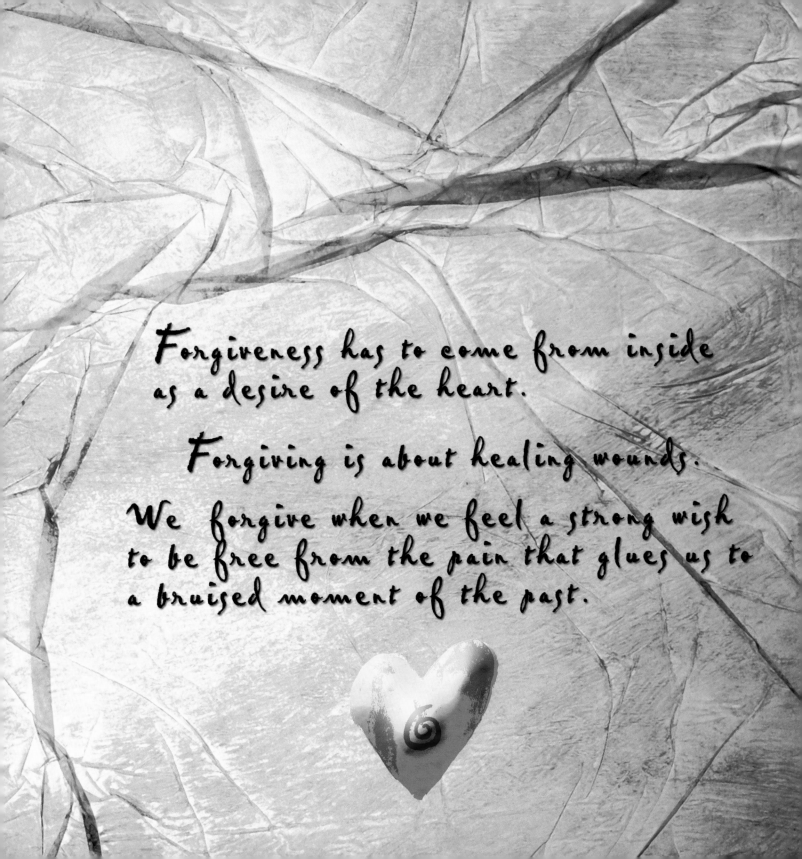

My Life Is A Wellspring Of Gratitude.

"Life will bring you pain all by itself.
Your responsibility is to create Joy."

Milton Erickson

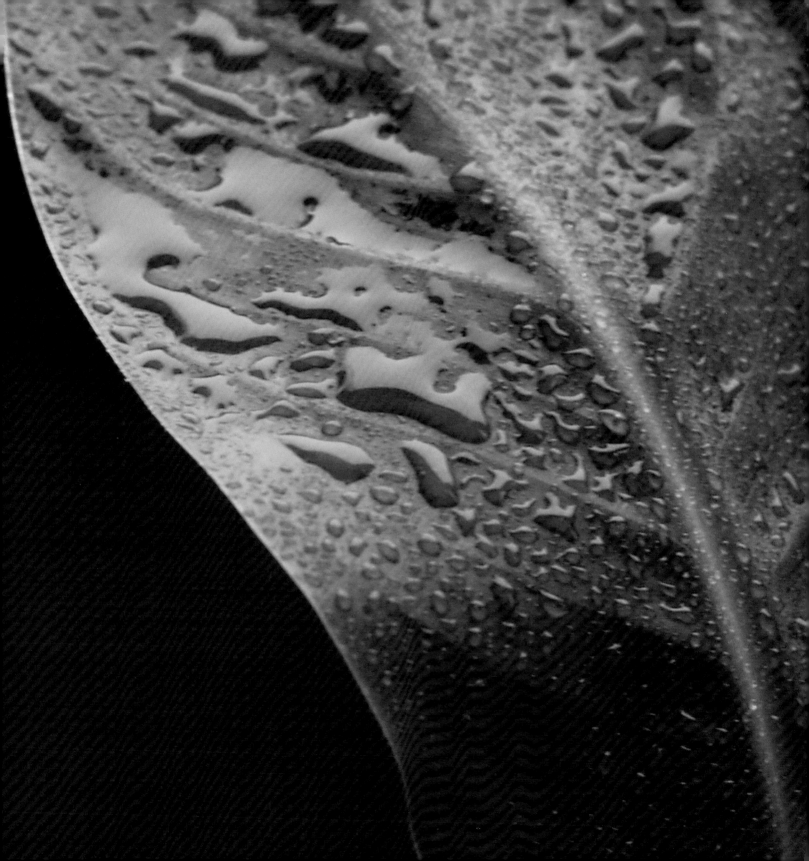

SOUL QUESTIONS

What hornets nest will you stir by making a change?

What does a significant life look like to you?

What keeps you from **living in the present moment?**

If today was your last day and you looked back on your life, **what would you say about it?**

What part of your life could use some forgiveness?

What do you need to release in order to access your joy?

What proactive choice could you make today that would have **a meaningful impact** on your life?

How long does it take to change your story?

You can change it in an instant.

Why do it?

To get your life back.

ABOUT THE AUTHOR

SOCRATES GOMEZ

John Drury is the author of **"Awaken Your Soul: A Journey of Discovery"** (2006), and the founder of his business. John believes that great Leaders lead from the inside out. **The Inside Out Edge** is an organization that inspires and guides current and aspiring Leaders to tap into their authentic power and potential as they navigate their Leadership Journey.

John resides in Fort Lauderdale, Florida, and has been married to his wife Debbie for 37 years. He has two beautiful daughters: Lauren and Jennie and two delicious grand daughters: Isabella and Gabriella.